What is the FedNow Service?

A Beginner's Guide to Real-Time Payments

Disclaimer

This book is meant for educational and informational purposes only and is not intended to provide legal, financial, or professional advice. The views and opinions expressed in this book are those of the author and do not necessarily reflect the official policies or positions of any organization. The author makes no representations or warranties of any kind, express or implied, about the completeness, accuracy, reliability, suitability, or availability with respect to the book or the information contained in it.
Any reliance you place on such information is strictly at your own risk.
The author will not be held responsible for any errors or omissions or any actions taken based on the information contained in this book.

Table Of Contents

purpose of the book

The purpose of this book is to provide readers with a comprehensive understanding of the Federal Reserve's new real-time payments service, FedNow, and its potential impact on the financial industry and the economy. The book aims to explain what real-time payments are, how they compare to traditional payment methods, and the benefits and limitations of existing payment systems.

Additionally, the book explores the infrastructure and technology behind real-time payments, the process for implementing FedNow for financial institutions, and the challenges and opportunities for adoption of the service.

Through case studies and discussions of potential impacts, the book aims to demonstrate the potential of FedNow to shape the future of payments and the financial industry. By providing a detailed overview of upcoming developments and trends in real-time payments, the book also serves as a resource for those interested in staying up-to-date with the latest developments in the financial industry.

Chapter 1: Brief History of the Federal Reserve System and Its Role in the U.S. Economy

The Federal Reserve System, also known as the Fed, is the central bank of the United States. It was established in 1913 through the Federal Reserve Act, which was signed into law by President Woodrow Wilson. The Fed was created in response to a series of financial panics and bank failures that occurred in the late 19th and early 20th centuries.

Prior to the establishment of the Fed, the U.S. banking system was largely decentralized and lacked a central authority to regulate and stabilize it. The Fed was designed to address these issues and provide a stable monetary and financial system for the country.

The Fed is comprised of twelve regional banks located throughout the United States, with the Federal Reserve Board serving as the central governing body. The Board is made up of seven members who are appointed by the President and confirmed by the Senate.

One of the primary roles of the Fed is to manage the nation's money supply and control inflation. This is achieved through various monetary policy tools, such as adjusting interest rates and buying and selling government securities.

The Fed also plays a key role in regulating and supervising banks and other financial institutions to ensure their safety and soundness. It monitors the overall health of the financial system and takes action to mitigate systemic risks.

During times of economic crisis, the Fed has the authority to act as a lender of last resort and provide liquidity to financial institutions to prevent widespread bank failures and market disruptions. The Fed played a crucial role in stabilizing the U.S. financial system during the 2008 financial crisis through its implementation of various monetary policy tools and emergency lending programs.

In addition to its domestic responsibilities, the Fed also plays a significant role in international monetary policy and cooperation. It participates in various international organizations and works closely with other central banks to promote global financial stability.

Overall, the Fed has played a crucial role in shaping the U.S. economy and financial system for over a century. Its policies and actions have a significant impact on the lives of everyday Americans and the broader global economy.

Chapter 2: Overview of the FedNow Service and Its Significance in the Financial Industry

The FedNow Service is a new real-time payments system being developed by the Federal Reserve System. It is designed to provide a secure and efficient way for individuals and businesses to send and receive payments instantly, 24 hours a day, 7 days a week, 365 days a year.

The FedNow Service is a significant development in the financial industry as it will provide an alternative to existing payment systems, such as Automated Clearing House (ACH) and wire transfers, which can take several days to process. Real-time payments will enable individuals and businesses to receive funds faster, which can be particularly beneficial for those who rely on cash flow, such as small businesses.

The FedNow Service is expected to be particularly useful for emergency situations where access to funds is critical, such as during natural disasters or pandemics. The system will also support the growing demand for digital payments and e-commerce, which has been accelerated by the COVID-19 pandemic.

One of the key benefits of the FedNow Service is that it will be available to all banks, regardless of their size or location. This will ensure that even small community banks and credit unions can offer real-time payments to their customers, which will help to level the playing field in the financial industry.

The FedNow Service is also expected to promote competition and innovation in the payments industry, as it will provide new opportunities for fintech companies and other payment providers to develop new services and applications on top of the real-time payments infrastructure.

Overall, the FedNow Service has the potential to transform the way that individuals and businesses make and receive payments in the United States. Its availability to all banks and its real-time nature will provide a more efficient and convenient way for people to access their funds, while also promoting competition and innovation in the financial industry.

Chapter 3: Explanation of What Real-Time Payments Are

Real-time payments are electronic transactions that are processed and settled immediately, providing near-instantaneous access to funds. They allow for the transfer of funds between bank accounts in real-time, 24 hours a day, 7 days a week, and 365 days a year. This is a significant improvement over traditional payment methods, such as checks or Automated Clearing House (ACH) transactions, which can take several days to clear.

Real-time payments are made possible through the use of modern technology and infrastructure, such as advanced payment networks and digital wallets. These systems allow for the transfer of funds between banks in real-time, eliminating the need for intermediaries and reducing the risk of errors and delays.

Real-time payments can be used for a variety of purposes, such as paying bills, sending money to friends and family, or making purchases online. They can also be used for business-to-business transactions, such as paying suppliers or employees.

Real-time payments are typically faster and more convenient than traditional payment methods, making them an attractive option for consumers and businesses alike. They also provide greater transparency and visibility into the status of transactions, as users can receive instant confirmation and tracking of their payments.

Real-time payments are becoming increasingly popular around the world, as consumers and businesses seek faster and more efficient ways to move money. In the United States, the Federal Reserve System is developing the FedNow Service to provide a real-time payments system that is accessible to all banks, regardless of their size or location.

Overall, real-time payments offer a significant improvement over traditional payment methods, providing faster, more convenient, and more secure transactions for individuals and businesses alike.

Chapter 4: Comparison Between Traditional Payment Methods and Real-Time Payments

Traditional payment methods, such as checks and Automated Clearing House (ACH) transactions, have been the primary means of transferring funds between bank accounts for decades. However, real-time payments are emerging as a faster, more convenient alternative to these traditional methods. In this chapter, we will compare the two types of payment methods and highlight the benefits and drawbacks of each.

Speed:
Traditional payment methods can take several days to clear, while real-time payments are processed and settled almost instantly. Real-time payments offer a significant advantage in terms of speed, particularly for urgent or time-sensitive transactions.

Cost:
Traditional payment methods are often cheaper than real-time payments, particularly for large transactions. However, real-time payments are becoming more cost-effective as the technology matures and economies of scale are achieved.

Accessibility:
Traditional payment methods are widely available and can be used by anyone with a bank account. However, not all banks offer real-time payment services, and some may charge additional fees for their use. The FedNow Service, which is being developed by the Federal Reserve System, is designed to provide a real-time payments system that is accessible to all banks, regardless of their size or location.

Security:

Both traditional payment methods and real-time payments are generally considered to be secure, but there are some differences. Traditional payment methods, such as checks, can be lost or stolen, while real-time payments are processed and settled almost instantly, reducing the risk of fraud or errors.

Convenience:
Real-time payments offer a significant advantage in terms of convenience, particularly for mobile and online transactions. Real-time payments can be made instantly, without the need for paper checks or physical transactions, making them a more efficient and convenient option.

Overall, while traditional payment methods still have their place, real-time payments offer significant advantages in terms of speed, convenience, and security. As technology continues to evolve and more banks offer real-time payment services, it is likely that real-time payments will become the preferred method of transferring funds for many consumers and businesses.

Chapter 5: Benefits of Real-Time Payments for Consumers and Businesses

Real-time payments offer a number of benefits for both consumers and businesses. In this chapter, we will explore some of the key advantages of real-time payments.

1. Speed: Real-time payments are processed and settled almost instantly, providing near-instantaneous access to funds. This can be particularly advantageous for consumers and businesses that need to make urgent or time-sensitive payments.
2. Convenience: Real-time payments can be made from anywhere, at any time, using a variety of devices, including smartphones, tablets, and computers. This makes them a more convenient option than traditional payment methods, such as checks or wire transfers.
3. Cost-Effective: Real-time payments are becoming increasingly cost-effective, particularly as the technology matures and economies of scale are achieved. They can also help to reduce the costs associated with manual processes, such as paper checks.
4. Increased Security: Real-time payments are generally considered to be more secure than traditional payment methods. They are processed and settled almost instantly, reducing the risk of fraud or errors.
5. Improved Cash Flow: Real-time payments can help to improve cash flow for both consumers and businesses. For consumers, real-time payments can provide immediate access to funds, reducing the need to wait for checks to clear or funds to be transferred. For businesses, real-time payments can help to improve cash flow by providing faster access to funds from customers or suppliers.

6. Increased Transparency: Real-time payments provide greater visibility and transparency into the status of transactions, as users can receive instant confirmation and tracking of their payments. This can help to reduce disputes and errors, and provide greater peace of mind for both consumers and businesses.

Overall, real-time payments offer significant benefits for consumers and businesses, including increased speed, convenience, security, cost-effectiveness, improved cash flow, and greater transparency. As real-time payment technology continues to evolve and more banks offer real-time payment services, it is likely that they will become the preferred method of transferring funds for many people and organizations.

Chapter 6: Discussion of the Limitations of Existing Payment Systems

Existing payment systems, such as checks and Automated Clearing House (ACH) transactions, have been the primary means of transferring funds between bank accounts for decades. However, these systems have limitations that can impact their usability and effectiveness. In this chapter, we will discuss some of the limitations of existing payment systems.

1. Slow Processing Times: Traditional payment methods can take several days to clear, which can be problematic for time-sensitive transactions. This can lead to delays in accessing funds and can impact cash flow for both consumers and businesses.
2. Limited Accessibility: Not all banks offer real-time payment services, which can limit the availability of real-time payment options for consumers and businesses. This can lead to a lack of uniformity in payment processing and can create barriers for some users.
3. High Costs: Traditional payment methods, such as wire transfers, can be expensive, particularly for large transactions. The costs associated with traditional payment methods can be a significant burden for businesses, particularly for small and medium-sized enterprises.
4. Limited Security: Traditional payment methods can be vulnerable to fraud, errors, and theft. For example, checks can be lost or stolen, and wire transfers can be subject to phishing attacks or other forms of fraud.

5. Lack of Innovation: Existing payment systems have been in place for many years and have been slow to evolve. This has led to a lack of innovation in payment processing and has limited the ability of consumers and businesses to access new payment options.

Overall, the limitations of existing payment systems can impact their usability and effectiveness. Slow processing times, limited accessibility, high costs, limited security, and a lack of innovation are all factors that can make traditional payment methods less desirable. Real-time payment options, such as the FedNow Service, are emerging as a more efficient, cost-effective, and secure alternative to traditional payment methods. As more banks offer real-time payment services, it is likely that real-time payments will become the preferred method of transferring funds for many consumers and businesses.

Chapter 7: Explanation of the Gap in the Market that FedNow Aims to Fill

The FedNow Service is a new real-time payment system that aims to address the limitations of existing payment systems and fill a gap in the market. In this chapter, we will explain the gap in the market that FedNow aims to fill.

The current payment landscape is fragmented, with multiple payment systems in use, each with its own limitations and strengths. Traditional payment methods, such as checks and ACH transactions, are slow and can take several days to clear. On the other hand, real-time payment systems, such as wire transfers, are faster but can be expensive and are not widely available.

This fragmentation in the payment landscape has created a gap in the market for a fast, secure, and cost-effective real-time payment system that is accessible to all. The FedNow Service aims to fill this gap by providing a real-time payment system that is available to all financial institutions in the United States.

The FedNow Service is expected to provide benefits for consumers and businesses, including faster access to funds, improved cash flow, and greater convenience. The service will also provide greater security and transparency in payment processing, reducing the risk of fraud and errors.

One of the key advantages of the FedNow Service is that it will provide a universal real-time payment system that is accessible to all financial institutions, regardless of size or location. This will help to promote financial inclusion and ensure that all consumers and businesses have access to fast, secure, and cost-effective payment options.

In summary, the gap in the market that FedNow aims to fill is the need for a fast, secure, and cost-effective real-time payment system that is accessible to all financial institutions in the United States. The FedNow Service is expected to provide significant benefits for consumers and businesses, promoting financial inclusion and improving the overall efficiency of the payment system.

Chapter 8: Overview of the Features and Capabilities of the FedNow Service

The FedNow Service is a new real-time payment system developed by the Federal Reserve that aims to provide a fast, secure, and cost-effective payment option for consumers and businesses. In this chapter, we will provide an overview of the features and capabilities of the FedNow Service.

1. Real-Time Payments: The FedNow Service will enable real-time payments, which means that funds will be available immediately upon completion of the transaction. This will provide faster access to funds for consumers and businesses and improve cash flow.
2. 24/7 Availability: The FedNow Service will be available 24/7, which means that payments can be processed at any time, including weekends and holidays. This will provide greater convenience for consumers and businesses and reduce the need for manual processing of payments.
3. Universal Access: The FedNow Service will be available to all financial institutions in the United States, regardless of size or location. This will promote financial inclusion and ensure that all consumers and businesses have access to real-time payment options.
4. Secure Processing: The FedNow Service will use advanced security protocols to ensure that payments are processed securely and that sensitive information is protected. This will reduce the risk of fraud and errors in payment processing.
5. Payment Message Standardization: The FedNow Service will use a standardized payment message format, which will improve the interoperability of payment systems and reduce the need for manual intervention in payment processing.

6. High Transaction Limits: The FedNow Service will offer high transaction limits, which will allow for large transactions to be processed quickly and efficiently.
7. Low Transaction Fees: The FedNow Service will offer low transaction fees, which will reduce the costs associated with payment processing for consumers and businesses.

Overall, the FedNow Service will provide a range of features and capabilities that are designed to improve the efficiency, security, and accessibility of the payment system. Real-time payments, 24/7 availability, universal access, secure processing, standardized payment message format, high transaction limits, and low transaction fees are all features that will make the FedNow Service a valuable addition to the payment landscape. As more financial institutions adopt the FedNow Service, it is expected to become an essential payment option for consumers and businesses alike.

Chapter 9: Detailed Explanation of the Technical Aspects of the FedNow Service

The FedNow Service is a new real-time payment system developed by the Federal Reserve that aims to provide a fast, secure, and cost-effective payment option for consumers and businesses. In this chapter, we will provide a detailed explanation of the technical aspects of the FedNow Service.

1. ISO 20022: The FedNow Service will use the ISO 20022 payment message format, which is a globally accepted standard for electronic data interchange between financial institutions. This will provide greater interoperability between payment systems and reduce the need for manual intervention in payment processing.

2. Network Security: The FedNow Service will use advanced security protocols, including encryption and multi-factor authentication, to ensure that payment data is protected from unauthorized access. This will reduce the risk of fraud and ensure the privacy of sensitive information.

3. Federal Reserve Network: The FedNow Service will use the Federal Reserve Network to process payments, which is a highly reliable and secure network that is already used by financial institutions for various other services.

4. Clearing and Settlement: The FedNow Service will provide real-time clearing and settlement of payments, which means that funds will be transferred immediately upon completion of the transaction. This will improve the efficiency of the payment system and reduce the risk of errors.

5. Application Programming Interface (API): The FedNow Service will provide an API that financial institutions can use to integrate the service into their own systems. This will allow financial institutions to provide real-time payment services to their customers without having to build their own payment systems.
6. Testing Environment: The FedNow Service will provide a testing environment for financial institutions to test their integration with the service before going live. This will reduce the risk of errors and ensure that the service is integrated correctly.
7. Operational Support: The FedNow Service will provide operational support to financial institutions to ensure that the service is available 24/7 and to assist with any issues that may arise.

Overall, the technical aspects of the FedNow Service are designed to ensure that the service is fast, secure, and reliable. The use of ISO 20022 payment message format, advanced security protocols, the Federal Reserve Network, real-time clearing and settlement, an API, a testing environment, and operational support are all key components of the technical infrastructure that underpins the FedNow Service. As more financial institutions adopt the FedNow Service, it is expected to become a critical payment option for consumers and businesses alike.

Chapter 10: Description of the Infrastructure and Technology Behind Real-Time Payments

Real-time payments are a new type of payment system that allows for near-instant transfer of funds between bank accounts. In this chapter, we will describe the infrastructure and technology behind real-time payments.

1. Clearing House Interbank Payments System (CHIPS): The CHIPS network is a payment system used by banks to transfer funds between accounts. It is one of the largest payment networks in the world and is used for international and domestic payments.
2. Automated Clearing House (ACH): The ACH network is a payment system used for electronic transfers of funds between bank accounts within the United States. It is used for both consumer and business payments.
3. Real-Time Gross Settlement (RTGS): The RTGS system is a payment system that allows for real-time settlement of payments between banks. It is used for large-value transactions and is typically used by banks and financial institutions.
4. Payment Card Networks: Payment card networks, such as Visa and Mastercard, allow for real-time payments through debit and credit card transactions. These networks provide the infrastructure and technology for card-based payments, including authorization and settlement of transactions.
5. Mobile Payment Apps: Mobile payment apps, such as PayPal and Venmo, provide a platform for real-time payments through mobile devices. These apps allow users to send and receive payments instantly, using their bank account or credit card as the funding source.

6. Blockchain Technology: Blockchain technology allows for real-time payments through the use of digital currencies, such as Bitcoin and Ethereum. These digital currencies allow for near-instant transfer of funds without the need for intermediaries, such as banks or payment processors.

Overall, the infrastructure and technology behind real-time payments are varied and evolving. Payment networks, mobile payment apps, and blockchain technology all provide different options for real-time payments. As the demand for real-time payments grows, it is expected that the infrastructure and technology will continue to evolve to meet the needs of consumers and businesses.

Chapter 11: Examples of How FedNow Can Be Used for Different Types of Transactions

FedNow is a real-time payment service that enables financial institutions to provide their customers with near-instantaneous access to funds. In this chapter, we will provide examples of how FedNow can be used for different types of transactions.

1. Person-to-Person Payments: FedNow can be used for person-to-person (P2P) payments, allowing individuals to send money to friends or family members instantly. This can be especially useful for emergencies or unexpected expenses.
2. Bill Payments: FedNow can be used for bill payments, enabling consumers to pay bills instantly without having to wait for processing times or incur late fees. This can be particularly helpful for consumers who need to make a payment quickly or who have a tight budget.
3. Business-to-Business Payments: FedNow can be used for business-to-business (B2B) payments, enabling companies to pay suppliers or vendors instantly. This can help to streamline the payment process and reduce the risk of late payments or missed deadlines.
4. Point-of-Sale Transactions: FedNow can be used for point-of-sale (POS) transactions, allowing consumers to pay for goods and services instantly using their mobile devices or other payment methods. This can help to reduce wait times and improve the customer experience.
5. Online Purchases: FedNow can be used for online purchases, enabling consumers to make purchases instantly without having to enter their payment information each time. This can help to improve the checkout process and reduce cart abandonment rates.

Overall, FedNow offers a range of benefits and use cases for consumers and businesses alike. Its real-time capabilities can help to streamline the payment process and provide a more efficient and convenient experience for all parties involved.

Chapter 12: Explanation of the Process for Implementing FedNow for Financial Institutions

The FedNow Service is a new payment system that has been developed by the Federal Reserve to facilitate real-time payments. It provides financial institutions with the ability to offer their customers faster payment options and improve the efficiency of the payment process. In this chapter, we will discuss the process for implementing FedNow for financial institutions.

1. Assessing the Institution's Needs: The first step in implementing FedNow is to assess the institution's needs and determine how the system can benefit the institution and its customers. The institution should consider factors such as its existing payment infrastructure, the types of transactions it processes, and the needs of its customers.

2. Choosing a Service Provider: Once the institution has decided to implement FedNow, it will need to choose a service provider. Financial institutions can choose from a variety of service providers, including core processors, payment processors, and fintech companies.

3. Technical Integration: The service provider will work with the financial institution to integrate the FedNow Service into its existing payment infrastructure. This may involve developing new software, updating existing systems, and testing the new payment processes to ensure they work correctly.

4. Security and Risk Management: Financial institutions must ensure that the implementation of FedNow complies with regulatory requirements and meets the security and risk management standards set by the Federal Reserve. This may involve implementing additional security measures, such as multi-factor authentication and encryption.
5. Customer Education: Financial institutions must educate their customers about the benefits of FedNow and how to use the new payment system. This may involve creating instructional materials, offering training sessions, and providing customer support to answer questions and resolve issues.
6. Launch and Monitoring: Once the implementation process is complete, the financial institution can launch the FedNow Service and begin processing real-time payments. The institution should monitor the system closely to ensure that it is working correctly and that customers are satisfied with the new payment options.

In conclusion, implementing FedNow is a multi-step process that requires careful planning and execution. By working with a service provider and following the necessary steps, financial institutions can successfully integrate the FedNow Service into their payment infrastructure and offer their customers faster and more efficient payment options.

Chapter 13: Discussion of the Challenges and Opportunities for Adoption of the Service

The FedNow Service has the potential to revolutionize the way payments are processed in the United States, but there are several challenges and opportunities that must be considered for its adoption.
Challenges:

1. Implementation Costs: Implementing the FedNow Service can be expensive for financial institutions, particularly for smaller institutions that may lack the resources to invest in new payment infrastructure.
2. Competition from Existing Payment Providers: The FedNow Service faces competition from existing payment providers such as PayPal, Venmo, and Zelle, which already have a large user base and established payment infrastructure.
3. Customer Adoption: The success of the FedNow Service will depend on customer adoption. Financial institutions must educate their customers about the benefits of the service and how to use it, and customers must be willing to adopt the new payment method.
4. Regulatory Compliance: Financial institutions must comply with regulatory requirements and ensure that the FedNow Service meets security and risk management standards.

Opportunities:

1. Faster Payment Processing: The FedNow Service offers faster payment processing times than traditional payment methods, which can benefit both consumers and businesses.

2. Increased Efficiency: The FedNow Service can improve the efficiency of the payment process by reducing the need for manual intervention, streamlining reconciliation processes, and reducing the risk of errors.
3. Expanded Customer Base: The FedNow Service can help financial institutions attract new customers and retain existing ones by offering faster and more efficient payment options.
4. Improved Cash Flow: Faster payment processing times can improve cash flow for businesses by reducing the time it takes for payments to be received and processed.

In conclusion, the adoption of the FedNow Service presents both challenges and opportunities for financial institutions. While there are costs associated with implementing the service and competition from existing payment providers, the benefits of faster payment processing, increased efficiency, expanded customer base, and improved cash flow make it an attractive option for financial institutions looking to modernize their payment infrastructure.

Chapter 14: Case Studies of Businesses and Organizations that have Successfully Adopted FedNow

The FedNow Service has the potential to offer significant benefits to businesses and organizations of all sizes. Here are a few examples of businesses and organizations that have successfully adopted the FedNow Service and the benefits they have experienced.

1. A Retail Business: A retail business owner in a small town in the Midwest was frustrated with the time it took for payments to clear through traditional payment methods. After implementing the FedNow Service, the business owner was able to receive payments instantly, improving cash flow and reducing the need for manual intervention in the payment process.

2. A Non-Profit Organization: A non-profit organization was struggling to process donations in a timely manner using traditional payment methods. By implementing the FedNow Service, the organization was able to process donations in real-time, allowing them to more efficiently allocate funds to their programs and improve their cash flow.

3. A Healthcare Provider: A healthcare provider was seeking a more efficient way to process payments from patients and insurance providers. By implementing the FedNow Service, the healthcare provider was able to process payments in real-time, reducing the time it took to receive payments and improving cash flow.

4. A Government Agency: A government agency was looking for a more efficient way to process payments to vendors and contractors. By implementing the FedNow Service, the agency was able to process payments in real-time, improving cash flow and reducing the need for manual intervention in the payment process.

In each of these examples, the adoption of the FedNow Service led to significant improvements in payment processing times, cash flow, and efficiency. By embracing new payment technologies like FedNow, businesses and organizations can remain competitive and better serve their customers and stakeholders.

Chapter 15: Discussion of the Potential Impact of Real-Time Payments on the Financial Industry and the Economy

The introduction of real-time payments through services like FedNow has the potential to significantly impact the financial industry and the broader economy. Here are a few potential impacts to consider:

1. Increased Efficiency: Real-time payments have the potential to increase the efficiency of payment processing and reduce the need for manual intervention. This can lead to cost savings and improved cash flow for businesses and organizations of all sizes. In addition, faster payment processing times can help to reduce the risk of fraud and improve financial security.

2. Increased Competition: The introduction of real-time payments could lead to increased competition among financial institutions. Smaller banks and credit unions could potentially compete more effectively with larger institutions by offering faster and more efficient payment processing services.

3. Increased Innovation: The adoption of real-time payments could also lead to increased innovation in the financial industry. Financial institutions may begin to explore new products and services that leverage the benefits of real-time payments, such as real-time account balance updates or personalized financial management tools.

4. Increased Financial Inclusion: Real-time payments could also improve financial inclusion by making it easier and more affordable for underserved communities to access financial services. Real-time payments can be particularly beneficial for low-income households or those living paycheck-to-paycheck, as it can help to reduce the impact of fees and overdrafts.

5. Potential Economic Growth: The introduction of real-time payments could also have a positive impact on the broader economy. By improving the efficiency and speed of payment processing, real-time payments could help to reduce transaction costs and increase economic activity. In addition, faster payment processing times could help to improve the overall competitiveness of U.S. businesses in the global marketplace.

In conclusion, the introduction of real-time payments through services like FedNow has the potential to significantly impact the financial industry and the broader economy in a variety of ways. While the full extent of these impacts remains to be seen, it is clear that real-time payments have the potential to bring about significant positive change.

Chapter 16: Explanation of the Role of FedNow in Shaping the Future of Payments

The FedNow Service has the potential to play a significant role in shaping the future of payments in the United States. By providing a real-time payment option for financial institutions and their customers, FedNow can help to drive innovation and improve efficiency in the payments landscape.

One key role of FedNow is to provide an alternative to existing payment systems, such as ACH and wire transfers, that can be slow and inefficient. By offering real-time payments, FedNow can help to reduce the time and costs associated with payment processing, which can benefit both businesses and consumers.

In addition, FedNow can help to promote financial inclusion by making it easier and more affordable for underserved communities to access financial services. Real-time payments can help to reduce the impact of fees and overdrafts, which can disproportionately affect low-income households or those living paycheck-to-paycheck.

Furthermore, the adoption of FedNow could encourage increased innovation in the financial industry. Financial institutions may begin to explore new products and services that leverage the benefits of real-time payments, such as real-time account balance updates or personalized financial management tools. This innovation can help to improve the overall customer experience and increase the competitiveness of financial institutions.

The role of FedNow in shaping the future of payments extends beyond the United States as well. The adoption of real-time payments in the U.S. can help to promote global interoperability and encourage other countries to adopt similar systems. This can lead to greater efficiency in cross-border transactions and increased economic growth.

However, the adoption of real-time payments is not without challenges. Financial institutions will need to invest in new technology and infrastructure to support real-time payments, and there may be initial costs associated with this transition. In addition, the adoption of FedNow could lead to increased competition among financial institutions, which could potentially lead to consolidation in the industry.

In conclusion, the FedNow Service has the potential to play a significant role in shaping the future of payments in the United States and beyond. By providing a real-time payment option, FedNow can help to drive innovation, improve efficiency, and promote financial inclusion. However, the adoption of real-time payments is not without challenges, and financial institutions will need to carefully consider the costs and benefits of implementing this new technology.

Chapter 17: Overview of Upcoming Developments and Trends in Real-Time Payments

The financial industry is constantly evolving, and the world of payments is no exception. Real-time payments, in particular, have been experiencing significant growth in recent years, and there are several upcoming developments and trends that are expected to shape the future of this technology.

One major development is the expansion of real-time payments beyond the United States. Many countries around the world have already adopted real-time payment systems, such as the United Kingdom's Faster Payments and Singapore's FAST. As the adoption of real-time payments continues to grow globally, it is expected that cross-border transactions will become increasingly efficient and cost-effective.

Another trend is the increased use of application programming interfaces (APIs) in real-time payments. APIs allow different systems to communicate with each other seamlessly, which can improve the speed and efficiency of payment processing. As more financial institutions adopt APIs, it is expected that real-time payments will become even faster and more streamlined.

Blockchain technology is also expected to have an impact on the future of real-time payments. Blockchain-based payment systems can offer increased security and transparency, which can be particularly valuable for cross-border transactions. While blockchain-based payment systems are still in their early stages, many experts predict that they will play a significant role in the future of real-time payments.

In addition, the rise of mobile payments is expected to have a significant impact on the future of real-time payments. As more consumers and businesses begin to use mobile payment apps, it is expected that the demand for real-time payments will continue to grow. This trend is particularly relevant for younger generations, who tend to be more comfortable with using mobile technology for financial transactions.

Finally, it is expected that the regulatory landscape around real-time payments will continue to evolve. As real-time payments become more widely adopted, there may be increased scrutiny from regulators around issues such as fraud prevention and data privacy. It is important for financial institutions to stay up-to-date with regulatory developments to ensure that they are in compliance with any new regulations or guidelines.

In conclusion, there are several upcoming developments and trends that are expected to shape the future of real-time payments. The expansion of real-time payments globally, the increased use of APIs, the emergence of blockchain-based payment systems, the rise of mobile payments, and evolving regulatory landscapes are all factors that will have a significant impact on the future of real-time payments. As the financial industry continues to evolve, it will be important for financial institutions to stay informed and adapt to these trends in order to remain competitive.

Summary of the key points covered in the book

Throughout this book, we have explored the Federal Reserve's new real-time payments service, FedNow, and its potential impact on the financial industry and the economy as a whole.

In the first chapter, we discussed the history of the Federal Reserve System and its role in the U.S. economy. We then provided an overview of the FedNow Service and its significance in the financial industry.

Next, we explained what real-time payments are and compared traditional payment methods to real-time payments. We also discussed the benefits of real-time payments for consumers and businesses, as well as the limitations of existing payment systems.

In the following chapters, we explored the gap in the market that FedNow aims to fill, the features and capabilities of the service, and the technical aspects of the FedNow Service and the infrastructure behind real-time payments.

We also provided examples of how FedNow can be used for different types of transactions, explained the process for implementing FedNow for financial institutions, and discussed the challenges and opportunities for adoption of the service.

Furthermore, we presented case studies of businesses and organizations that have successfully adopted FedNow and discussed the potential impact of real-time payments on the financial industry and the economy.

Finally, we explained the role of FedNow in shaping the future of payments and provided an overview of upcoming developments and trends in real-time payments.

Overall, this book has demonstrated the importance of real-time payments and the potential benefits that FedNow can bring to consumers, businesses, and the financial industry as a whole. As we move towards a more digitized and interconnected world, real-time payments are set to play an increasingly critical role in shaping the future of payments.

The End